VECTOR DATABASE

A PRACTICAL GUIDE TO BUILDING INTELLIGENT SEARCH APPLICATIONS

OLIVER LUCAS JR

TABLE OF CONTENTS

Chapter 7

Chapter 8

Chapter 9

Chapter 10

Chapter 1

Introduction to Vector Databases

1.1 What is a Vector Database?

A vector database is a specialized type of database designed to store and retrieve vector data efficiently. Vectors are mathematical representations of data points in a high-dimensional space. Each dimension in the vector corresponds to a specific feature or characteristic of the data.

Key Features of Vector Databases:

Vector Storage: Stores high-dimensional vectors, often representing complex data like images, text, or audio.

Similarity Search: Efficiently retrieves the most similar vectors to a given query vector.

Indexing: Creates indexes on vector data to accelerate search queries.

Scalability: Handles large datasets and high query loads.

Integration with Machine Learning: Works seamlessly with machine learning models to generate and process vector embeddings.

Common Use Cases:

Semantic Search: Enables searching for information based on meaning and context, rather than exact keywords.

Recommendation Systems: Recommends products, content, or other items based on user preferences and similarity.

Anomaly Detection: Identifies unusual patterns or outliers in data

Image and Video Search: Searches for similar images or videos based on visual content

Natural Language Processing: Understands and processes human language to perform tasks like sentiment analysis, text classification, and machine translation.

Popular Vector Databases:

Pinecone

Faiss

Milvus

Weaviate

Qdrant

By leveraging vector databases, organizations can unlock the power of their unstructured data and build intelligent applications that can understand and respond to complex queries.

1.2 Why Vector Databases Matter

Vector databases matter because they revolutionize how we interact with data, particularly in the age of artificial intelligence. Here's why:

1. Semantic Understanding:

Beyond Keywords: Traditional databases rely on exact keyword matches. Vector databases, on the other hand, understand the semantic meaning of data, allowing for more nuanced and relevant searches.

Contextual Relevance: They can find information based on context, not just keywords. This enables more accurate and insightful search results.

2. Efficient Similarity Search:

High-Dimensional Data: Vector databases excel at handling high-dimensional data, making them ideal for complex data types like images, audio, and text.

Rapid Retrieval: They can quickly find the most similar data points to a given query, enabling real-time applications.

3. Powerful AI Applications

Semantic Search: Build powerful search engines that understand user intent and provide relevant results.

Recommendation Systems: Create personalized recommendations based on user preferences and behavior.

Anomaly Detection: Identify unusual patterns in data, helping prevent fraud and security breaches

Natural Language Processing: Understand and process human language, enabling tasks like sentiment analysis, text summarization, and machine translation.

4. Scalability and Performance:

Handling Large Datasets: Vector databases are designed to handle massive amounts of data efficiently.

Real-time Insights: They can process queries in real-time, enabling fast and responsive applications.

In essence, vector databases empower us to unlock the full potential of our data, leading to more intelligent, efficient, and innovative applications.

1.3 Key Concepts and Terminology in Vector Databases

Here are some key concepts and terms you'll encounter when working with vector databases:

Fundamental Concepts:

Vector: A mathematical representation of data points in a multi-dimensional space. Each dimension corresponds to a specific feature or attribute of the data.

Vector Embedding: A technique to map complex data (like text, images, or audio) into a numerical vector representation.

Similarity Search: The process of finding the most similar vectors to a given query vector.

Vector Database Terminology:

Vector Index: A data structure that organizes vectors for efficient similarity search.

Approximate Nearest Neighbors (ANN): Algorithms used to find approximate nearest neighbors of a query vector, often used in large-scale datasets.

Vector Similarity Metrics: Functions used to measure the similarity between two vectors, such as Euclidean distance, cosine similarity, or Jaccard similarity.

Vector Quantization: A technique to reduce the dimensionality of vectors while preserving their semantic meaning.

Additional Concepts:

Metadata: Additional information associated with a vector, such as timestamps, labels, or categories.

Hybrid Search: Combining traditional keyword-based search with vector-based semantic search.

Pipeline: A sequence of steps involved in processing data, from data ingestion to vectorization and indexing.

By understanding these concepts, you can effectively leverage vector databases to build powerful AI applications.

Chapter 2

Understanding Vector Embeddings

2.1 The Basics of Embeddings

What are Embeddings?

Embeddings are numerical representations of words, phrases, or even entire documents in a high-dimensional space. These representations are designed to capture semantic and syntactic relationships between words and phrases. In simpler terms, embeddings allow machines to understand the meaning and context of language.

Why are Embeddings Important?

Semantic Similarity: Embeddings enable machines to understand the similarity between words and phrases. Words with similar meanings will have similar embeddings. For example, the embeddings for "cat" and "feline" will be closer to each other than the embeddings for "cat" and "table."

Contextual Understanding: Embeddings can capture the context of words. The same word can have different meanings in different contexts. For instance, the word "bank" can refer to a financial institution or the side of a river. Embeddings can differentiate between these two meanings based on the surrounding words.

Machine Learning Applications: Embeddings are essential for various machine learning tasks, including:

Text Classification: Categorizing text documents into predefined categories.

Sentiment Analysis: Determining the sentiment (positive, negative, or neutral) of text.

Machine Translation: Translating text from one language to another.

Text Generation: Generating human-quality text.

Information Retrieval: Finding relevant information from large datasets.

How are Embeddings Created?

Embeddings are typically created using neural networks, such as:

Word Embeddings:

Word2Vec: A technique that learns word embeddings by analyzing the context of words in a large corpus of text.

GloVe: A technique that learns word embeddings by considering the co-occurrence of words in a corpus.

Contextual Embeddings:

BERT (Bidirectional Encoder Representations from Transformers): A powerful language model that can generate context-aware embeddings for words and phrases.

GPT-3: A large language model capable of generating human-quality text and understanding complex language.

By understanding the basics of embeddings, you can leverage their power to build intelligent applications that can understand and process human language.

2.2 Popular Embedding Techniques

Here are some of the most popular embedding techniques used in natural language processing and machine learning:

Word Embeddings

Word2Vec: This technique trains a neural network model on a large text corpus to learn word associations. It produces dense vector representations of words, capturing semantic and syntactic similarities.

GloVe (Global Vectors for Word Representation): GloVe combines the advantages of matrix factorization and local context window methods. It leverages global word-word co-occurrence statistics to learn word embeddings.

Contextual Embeddings

BERT (Bidirectional Encoder Representations from Transformers): BERT is a powerful language model that can generate context-aware embeddings for words and phrases. It considers the entire context of a sentence to produce more accurate embeddings.

GPT-3 (Generative Pre-trained Transformer 3): GPT-3 is a large language model capable of generating human-quality text and understanding complex language. It can also be used to generate context-aware embeddings.

RoBERTa (Robustly Optimized BERT Pretraining Approach): RoBERTa is a more robust version of BERT, trained on a larger dataset and with more training steps.

XLNet: XLNet is a generalized autoregressive pretraining method that outperforms BERT on many natural language understanding tasks.

Other Techniques

FastText: This technique extends word embeddings to subword-level information, making it suitable for handling rare words and out-of-vocabulary words.

ELMo (Embeddings from Language Models): ELMo is a contextual embedding technique that combines static word embeddings with character-level representations.

By understanding these embedding techniques, you can choose the best approach for your specific natural language processing task and achieve better results.

2.3 Evaluating Embedding Quality

Evaluating the quality of embeddings is crucial for ensuring that they effectively capture semantic and syntactic relationships between words and phrases. Here are some common methods for evaluating embedding quality:

Intrinsic Evaluation

Intrinsic evaluation assesses the quality of embeddings directly, without relying on downstream tasks. This involves tasks like:

Word Similarity: Measuring how well embeddings capture semantic similarity between words.

Cosine Similarity: Calculate the cosine similarity between the embeddings of two words. A higher cosine similarity indicates a greater semantic similarity.

Word Similarity Datasets: Use datasets like WordSim353 or SimLex-999 to evaluate word similarity.

Word Analogy: Testing the ability of embeddings to solve word analogy problems, such as "king is to queen as man is to woman."

Embedding Visualization: Visualizing embeddings in a 2D or 3D space can help identify clusters of semantically similar words.

Extrinsic Evaluation

Extrinsic evaluation assesses the quality of embeddings indirectly by measuring their performance on downstream tasks, such as:

Text Classification: Using embeddings as features for text classification tasks like sentiment analysis or topic classification.

Machine Translation: Using embeddings to improve the quality of machine translation systems.

Information Retrieval: Using embeddings to enhance information retrieval systems by improving the ranking of relevant documents.

Question Answering: Using embeddings to improve the accuracy of question-answering systems.

Other Considerations

Dimensionality: The dimensionality of embeddings can impact their quality. Higher-dimensional embeddings can capture more complex relationships, but they may also be more computationally expensive.

Training Data: The quality of the training data used to train the embedding model can significantly impact the quality of the resulting embeddings.

Model Architecture: The architecture of the neural network used to train the embeddings can also affect their quality.

By combining intrinsic and extrinsic evaluation methods, we can gain a comprehensive understanding of the quality of embeddings and make informed decisions about their use in various applications.

Chapter 3

Building a Vector Database

3.1 Choosing the Right Vector Database

When selecting a vector database, consider the following factors:

Key Considerations:

Performance:

Query Latency: How quickly can the database retrieve relevant vectors?

Throughput: How many queries can the database handle per second?

Scalability: Can the database handle increasing data volumes and query loads?

Features:

Similarity Search: Does it support efficient similarity search techniques like approximate nearest neighbors (ANN)?

Indexing Techniques: Does it offer various indexing techniques to optimize search performance?

Vector Formats: Does it support different vector formats (e.g., dense, sparse)?

Metadata Support: Can it store additional metadata with vectors?

Integration:

API and SDKs: Does it provide easy-to-use APIs and SDKs for different programming languages?

Cloud Integration: Can it be easily integrated with cloud platforms like AWS, GCP, or Azure?

Cost:

Licensing Costs: Are there licensing fees or usage-based costs?

Infrastructure Costs: What are the infrastructure costs (e.g., hardware, cloud resources)?

Security and Privacy:

Data Encryption: Does it offer data encryption at rest and in transit?

Access Controls: Can you control access to the database and its data?

Compliance: Does it comply with relevant data privacy regulations (e.g., GDPR, CCPA)?

Popular Vector Database Options:

Pinecone:

Cloud-native, highly scalable, and easy to use.

Offers advanced features like hybrid search and filtering.

Faiss:

Open-source library for efficient similarity search.

Highly customizable and optimized for performance.

Requires more technical expertise to set up and manage.

Milvus:

Open-source vector database with a focus on scalability and performance.

Supports a variety of data types and indexing techniques.

Weaviate:

Semantic search engine that combines vector search with knowledge graph capabilities.

Allows you to create schemas and define relationships between concepts.

Qdrant:

Fast and scalable vector database with advanced filtering and ranking capabilities.

Supports hybrid search and offers a user-friendly API.

Choosing the Right Database for Your Use Case

Consider the specific requirements of your application:

Simple Semantic Search: Pinecone or Weaviate might be good choices.

Complex AI Applications: Faiss or Milvus offer more flexibility and control.

Real-time Analytics: Qdrant's fast query performance could be beneficial.

By carefully evaluating these factors and considering your specific needs, you can select the most suitable vector database for your project.

3.2 Setting Up a Vector Database

Here's a general guide on setting up a vector database. The specific steps may vary depending on the chosen database:

1. Choose a Vector Database:

Cloud-Based: Pinecone, Weaviate, or Qdrant are popular cloud-based options.

Self-Hosted: Faiss or Milvus can be deployed on your own infrastructure.

2. Set Up the Infrastructure:

Cloud-Based: Create an account and follow the provider's instructions to set up a new index.

Self-Hosted:

Hardware: Ensure sufficient CPU, RAM, and storage.

Software: Install the database software and dependencies.

Configuration: Configure the database with appropriate settings for your workload.

3. Prepare Your Data:

Vectorization: Convert your data (text, images, audio) into numerical vectors using techniques like:

Word Embeddings: Word2Vec, GloVe, BERT

Image Embeddings: CLIP, ResNet

Audio Embeddings: VGGish, ResNe

Data Cleaning and Preprocessing: Clean and preprocess your data to improve embedding quality.

4. Ingest Data:

Batch Ingestion: Load large datasets in batches.

Stream Ingestion: Continuously ingest data in real-time.

API: Use the database's API to ingest data programmatically.

5. Create an Index:

Vector Index: Define the vector dimension and similarity metric (e.g., cosine similarity, Euclidean distance).

Metadata Index: Index metadata fields for filtering and sorting.

6. Perform Similarity Search:

Query Vector: Create a query vector representing the search query.

Similarity Search: Use the database's API to perform similarity search and retrieve the most similar vectors.

Example Using Pinecone:

Create a Pinecone Index:

Python

```python
import pinecone

# Initialize Pinecone
pinecone.init(
    api_key="YOUR_API_KEY",  # Replace with your API key
    environment="YOUR_ENVIRONMENT"  # Replace with your
environment
)

# Create an index
pinecone.create_index(
    name="my-index",
    dimension=128,  # Dimension of your vectors
    metric="CosineSimilarity"
)
```

Insert Vectors:
Python

```python
# Insert vectors with metadata
pinecone.upsert(
```

```
    index_name="my-index",
    vectors=[
        ("vector1", [1, 2, 3, ...]),
        ("vector2", [4, 5, 6, ...]),
        # ...
    ]
)
```

Query the Index:

Python

```
# Query the index
query_vector = [0.1, 0.2, 0.3, ...]
response = pinecone.query(
    index_name="my-index",
    vector=query_vector,
    top_k=10
)
```

Remember to adapt these steps to the specific database you choose and your particular use case.

3.3 Data Ingestion and Indexing in Vector Databases

Data Ingestion

Data ingestion is the process of loading your data into the vector database. This involves

Vectorization:

Text Data: Use techniques like Word2Vec, BERT, or other language models to convert text into numerical vectors.

Image Data: Employ image embedding models like CLIP or ResNet to extract visual features.

Audio Data: Use audio embedding models like VGGish or ResNet to extract audio features.

Data Preprocessing:

Cleaning: Remove noise, inconsistencies, and irrelevant information.

Normalization: Scale or standardize data to a common range.

Tokenization: Break text data into tokens (words or subwords).

Data Loading:

Batch Ingestion: Load large datasets in batches.

Stream Ingestion: Continuously ingest data in real-time.

API: Use the database's API to ingest data programmatically.

Indexing

Indexing is the process of creating data structures that allow for efficient search and retrieval of vectors.

Vector Index:

Approximate Nearest Neighbors (ANN): Algorithms like HNSW, IVF-PQ, and Annoy are used to efficiently find the nearest neighbors of a query vector.

Metric Space: The choice of distance metric (e.g., Euclidean distance, cosine similarity) impacts index performance.

Metadata Index:

Filtering: Index metadata fields to filter results based on specific criteria.

Sorting: Index metadata fields to sort results by certain attributes.

Example using Pinecone:

```python
Python
import pinecone

# Initialize Pinecone
pinecone.init(
    api_key="YOUR_API_KEY",
    environment="YOUR_ENVIRONMENT"
)

# Create an index
pinecone.create_index(
    name="my-index",
    dimension=128,  # Dimension of your vectors
    metric="CosineSimilarity"
)

# Insert vectors with metadata
pinecone.upsert(
    index_name="my-index",
    vectors=[
        ("vector1", [1, 2, 3, ...], {"metadata": {"category": "A"}}),
        ("vector2", [4, 5, 6, ...], {"metadata": {"category": "B"}}),
        # ...
    ]
)
```

Key Considerations:

Vector Dimensionality: Higher dimensions can capture more complex relationships but can also impact performance.

Index Type: Choose an appropriate index type based on your query patterns and data distribution.

Hardware and Software: Ensure sufficient resources to handle your workload.

Data Quality: Clean and well-prepared data leads to better search results.

Monitoring and Optimization: Monitor the performance of your vector database and optimize it as needed.

By effectively ingesting and indexing your data, you can unlock the full potential of your vector database and build powerful AI applications.

Chapter 4

Searching with Vector Databases

4.1 Similarity Search Techniques

Similarity search is a fundamental operation in vector databases, allowing us to find items that are similar to a given query. Here are some common techniques:

1. Exact Nearest Neighbor (ENN) Search

Brute Force: Directly calculates the distance between the query vector and every other vector in the database.

Suitable for: Small datasets or when exact results are crucial.

Inefficient for large datasets due to high computational cost.

2. Approximate Nearest Neighbor (ANN) Search

Approximates the nearest neighbors to reduce computational cost.

Popular Algorithms:

HNSW (Hierarchical Navigable Small World): Efficient for high-dimensional spaces and dynamic datasets.

IVFFlat (Inverted File Index Flat): Suitable for large datasets with moderate dimensionality.

Annoy (Approximate Nearest Neighbors Oh Yeah): Fast and easy to use, but less accurate than HNSW and IVFFlat.

3. Locality-Sensitive Hashing (LSH)

Groups similar vectors into buckets based on hash functions.

Efficient for approximate nearest neighbor search in high-dimensional spaces.

Less accurate than ANN algorithms for specific use cases.

4. Product Quantization (PQ)

Compresses vectors into smaller codewords.

Reduces storage and computational costs for similarity search.

Suitable for large-scale datasets with high-dimensional vectors.

Choosing the Right Technique

The choice of technique depends on several factors:

Dataset Size: For small datasets, exact nearest neighbor search might be sufficient. For large datasets, approximate nearest neighbor search is more efficient.

Vector Dimensionality: High-dimensional spaces often benefit from techniques like LSH and PQ.

Query Frequency: If queries are frequent, techniques like HNSW can provide fast response times.

Accuracy Requirements: If high accuracy is critical, exact nearest neighbor search or more accurate ANN algorithms are preferred.

Hardware Constraints: Consider the computational resources available and choose a technique that balances accuracy and efficiency.

By understanding these techniques and their trade-offs, you can effectively perform similarity search in your vector database applications.

4.2 Approximate Nearest Neighbors (ANN)

Approximate Nearest Neighbor (ANN) search is a technique used to efficiently find the closest data points in high-dimensional spaces. It's particularly useful for large datasets where exact nearest neighbor search (which checks every data point) becomes computationally expensive.

Why ANN?

Efficiency: ANN algorithms offer significant speedups compared to exact nearest neighbor search, especially for large datasets.

Scalability: They can handle high-dimensional data and large-scale datasets.

Approximation: While they don't guarantee the exact nearest neighbor, they often find very close approximations.

Popular ANN Algorithms:

HNSW (Hierarchical Navigable Small World):

Creates a hierarchical graph structure to efficiently navigate the search space.

Well-suited for high-dimensional spaces and dynamic datasets.

IVFFlat (Inverted File Index Flat):

Divides the dataset into clusters and creates an inverted index to quickly locate candidate points.

Efficient for large datasets with moderate dimensionality.

Annoy (Approximate Nearest Neighbors Oh Yeah):

Simple and fast algorithm that builds a forest of trees to approximate nearest neighbors.

Less accurate than HNSW and IVFFlat but easier to implement.

Applications of ANN:

Recommendation Systems: Finding similar items or users based on their features.

Image Search: Searching for visually similar images.

Natural Language Processing: Finding semantically similar words or documents.

Anomaly Detection: Identifying outliers in data.

Clustering: Grouping similar data points together.

Key Considerations for ANN:

Data Dimensionality: Higher-dimensional spaces require more sophisticated ANN algorithms.

Dataset Size: Large datasets may benefit from techniques like quantization to reduce memory usage.

Query Frequency: Frequent queries may require more efficient indexing structures.

Accuracy Requirements: The desired level of accuracy will influence the choice of algorithm and its parameters.

Hardware and Software: The computational resources and software libraries available can impact the choice of ANN algorithm.

By understanding the principles of ANN and the available algorithms, you can effectively apply them to various tasks involving similarity search in high-dimensional spaces.

4.3 Optimizing Search Performance in Vector Databases

Optimizing search performance in vector databases is crucial for ensuring efficient and accurate results, especially when dealing with large datasets and complex queries. Here are some key strategies to consider:

1. Index Selection and Tuning

Choose the Right Index: Select an appropriate index structure (e.g., HNSW, IVFFlat, Annoy) based on your dataset size, dimensionality, and query patterns.

Index Parameter Tuning: Experiment with different index parameters to find the optimal configuration.

Dynamic Indexing: Consider using dynamic indexing techniques to update the index as new data is added or existing data changes.

2. Vector Quantization

Reduce Vector Dimensionality: Apply techniques like PCA or t-SNE to reduce the dimensionality of your vectors while preserving important information.

Quantization: Quantize vectors to a lower precision to reduce storage and computation costs.

3. Query Optimization

Query Filtering: Use metadata filters to reduce the search space and improve query performance.

Query Vector Quality: Ensure that the query vector is accurate and representative of the desired search intent.

Batch Queries: Process multiple queries simultaneously to improve efficiency.

4. Hardware and Software Optimization

Hardware Acceleration: Utilize GPUs or specialized hardware accelerators to speed up computations.

Efficient Data Structures: Use efficient data structures and algorithms to minimize memory usage and CPU cycles.

Parallel Processing: Leverage parallel processing techniques to distribute the workload across multiple cores or machines.

5. Monitoring and Profiling

Monitor Query Performance: Track query latency, throughput, and error rates.

Identify Bottlenecks: Analyze system logs and performance metrics to identify performance bottlenecks.

Optimize Index and Query Strategies: Adjust index parameters and query strategies to improve performance.

6. Consider Hybrid Search Approaches

Keyword Search and Semantic Search: Combine keyword-based search with semantic search to improve accuracy and relevance.

Filtering and Ranking: Use filtering techniques to reduce the search space and ranking algorithms to prioritize relevant results.

By carefully considering these strategies and continuously monitoring and optimizing your vector database, you can achieve significant improvements in search performance, scalability, and accuracy.

Chapter 5

Semantic Search

5.1 Understanding Semantic Search

Semantic search is a search technology that goes beyond keyword matching to understand the meaning and context of a query. It leverages techniques like natural language processing (NLP) and machine learning to interpret the user's intent and provide more relevant results.

How does it work?

Textual Analysis: The query is broken down into its constituent parts, and their semantic meaning is extracted.

Vector Space Model: The query and documents in the database are represented as vectors in a high-dimensional space.

Similarity Search: The system calculates the similarity between the query vector and document vectors.

Ranking: The most similar documents are ranked and presented to the user.

Key Benefits of Semantic Search:

Improved Search Accuracy: Semantic search can understand synonyms, related terms, and context, leading to more accurate results.

Enhanced User Experience: It provides a more intuitive and natural search experience, reducing the need for precise keyword matching.

Better Understanding of User Intent: Semantic search can identify the underlying intent behind a query, even if it's expressed in different ways.

Advanced Search Capabilities: It enables features like question answering, summarization, and sentiment analysis.

Real-world Applications:

Enterprise Search: Finding relevant documents within a company's knowledge base.

E-commerce: Improving product search and recommendations.

Customer Service: Enhancing search capabilities in help centers and chatbots.

Content Management Systems: Facilitating content discovery and organization.

By leveraging the power of semantic search, organizations can improve information retrieval, enhance user experience, and drive better business outcomes.

5.2 Building a Semantic Search Engine

Building a semantic search engine involves several key steps:

1. Data Collection and Preprocessing:

Gather Data: Collect a large corpus of text data relevant to your domain.

Data Cleaning: Remove noise, inconsistencies, and irrelevant information.

Tokenization: Break text into tokens (words or subwords).

Stop Word Removal: Remove common words that don't add much meaning.

Stemming or Lemmatization: Reduce words to their root form.

2. Vectorization:

Word Embeddings: Use techniques like Word2Vec, GloVe, or BERT to convert words and phrases into numerical vectors.

Document Embeddings: Represent entire documents as vectors, often by averaging word embeddings or using more advanced techniques like sentence transformers.

3. Vector Database:

Choose a Vector Database: Select a suitable vector database like Pinecone, Faiss, Milvus, or Weaviate.

Index Creation: Create an index to store the vectors and their associated metadata.

Data Ingestion: Load the vectorized documents into the database.

4. Query Processing and Similarity Search:

Query Vectorization: Convert the user's query into a vector.

Similarity Search: Use the vector database to find the most similar documents to the query vector.

Ranking: Rank the results based on similarity scores and other factors like metadata.

5. Result Presentation:

Display Relevant Results: Present the top-ranked results to the user.

Highlight Relevant Passages: Highlight the most relevant parts of the documents.

Provide Contextual Information: Offer additional context or related information to enhance the search experience.

Key Technologies and Libraries:

NLP Libraries: NLTK, spaCy, Hugging Face Transformers

Vector Database: Pinecone, Faiss, Milvus, Weaviate

Machine Learning Frameworks: TensorFlow, PyTorch

Search Engines: Elasticsearch, Algolia

Example using Python and Pinecone:

```python
Python
import pinecone
from sentence_transformers import SentenceTransformer

# Initialize Pinecone
pinecone.init(
    api_key="YOUR_API_KEY",
    environment="YOUR_ENVIRONMENT"
)

# Create an index
pinecone.create_index(
    name="my-index",
    dimension=768,  # Dimension of sentence embeddings
```

```python
    metric="CosineSimilarity"
)

# Vectorize documents
model = SentenceTransformer('all-MiniLM-L6-v2')
embeddings = model.encode(["Document 1", "Document 2", ...])

# Insert vectors into Pinecone
pinecone.upsert(
    index_name="my-index",
    vectors=[
        ("doc1", embeddings[0]),
        ("doc2", embeddings[1]),
        # ...
    ]
)

# Query the index
query_vector = model.encode(["User query"])
results = pinecone.query(
    index_name="my-index",
    vector=query_vector,
    top_k=5
)
```

By following these steps and leveraging the power of advanced technologies, you can build robust and effective semantic search engines.

5.3 Enhancing Search Relevance in Semantic Search

To further enhance search relevance in semantic search, consider these strategies:

1. Contextual Understanding

Contextual Embeddings: Use language models like BERT or RoBERTa to capture the context of words and phrases.

Entity Recognition: Identify named entities (people, organizations, locations) to improve understanding.

Sentiment Analysis: Analyze the sentiment of the query and documents to refine results.

2. Query Expansion

Synonym Expansion: Expand the query with synonyms and related terms.

Semantic Expansion: Use knowledge graphs or semantic networks to identify related concepts.

3. Ranking and Re-ranking

Learning-to-Rank: Train machine learning models to rank search results based on relevance and user feedback.

Re-ranking: Re-rank the top results using additional factors like freshness, popularity, and user preferences.

4. Feedback Loop

User Feedback: Collect user feedback on search results to improve future queries.

Click-Through Rate (CTR): Analyze user behavior to identify relevant and irrelevant results.

A/B Testing: Experiment with different search algorithms and ranking strategies.

5. Hybrid Search

Combining Semantic and Keyword Search: Use semantic search for complex queries and keyword search for simple queries.

Filtering and Faceting: Allow users to filter and refine search results based on specific criteria.

6. Evaluation Metrics

Precision, Recall, F1-score: Evaluate the accuracy of the search results.

Mean Reciprocal Rank (MRR): Measure the ranking quality of the top-ranked relevant document.

Normalized Discounted Cumulative Gain (NDCG): Consider both relevance and ranking position.

By implementing these techniques, you can significantly improve the quality and relevance of semantic search results, providing a better user experience.

Would you like to delve deeper into a specific technique or discuss a particular use case?

Chapter 6

Recommendation Systems

6.1 Building Recommendation Systems with Vector Databases

Recommendation systems are a powerful tool to suggest relevant items to users. Vector databases can significantly enhance these systems by enabling efficient similarity search and personalized recommendations.

Key Steps in Building a Recommendation System:

Data Collection and Preparation:

User Data: Collect information about user preferences, demographics, and behavior.

Item Data: Gather details about items, such as descriptions, categories, and ratings.

Interaction Data: Record user-item interactions, like purchases, ratings, or clicks.

Feature Engineering:

User Features: Extract relevant features from user data, such as age, gender, and purchase history.

Item Features: Extract features from item data, such as genre, director, or keywords.

Contextual Features: Consider contextual factors like time, location, or device.

Vectorization:

User Embeddings: Represent users as vectors in a high-dimensional space.

Item Embeddings: Represent items as vectors.

Contextual Embeddings: Represent context as vectors.

Vector Database:

Store Embeddings: Store user and item embeddings in a vector database.

Similarity Search: Use similarity search techniques to find similar users or items.

Recommendation Algorithms:

Collaborative Filtering:

User-Based: Recommend items that similar users have liked.

Item-Based: Recommend items similar to those the user has interacted with.

Content-Based Filtering: Recommend items with similar features to those the user has liked.

Hybrid Approaches: Combine collaborative and content-based filtering for more accurate recommendations.

Evaluation:

Offline Evaluation: Use historical data to measure the accuracy of recommendations.

Online A/B Testing: Test different recommendation algorithms and strategies in a live environment.

Example using Pinecone:

```python
Python
import pinecone

# Initialize Pinecone
pinecone.init(
    api_key="YOUR_API_KEY",
    environment="YOUR_ENVIRONMENT"
)

# Create an index for items
pinecone.create_index(
    name="item_index",
    dimension=128,  # Dimension of item embeddings
    metric="CosineSimilarity"
)

# Insert item vectors
pinecone.upsert(
    index_name="item_index",
    vectors=[
        ("item1", [1, 2, 3, ...]),
        ("item2", [4, 5, 6, ...]),
        # ...
    ]
)

# Find similar items for a given item
query_vector = [0.1, 0.2, 0.3, ...]
results = pinecone.query(
    index_name="item_index",
    vector=query_vector,
```

```
    top_k=10
)
```

By leveraging vector databases and advanced recommendation algorithms, you can build powerful recommendation systems that provide personalized and relevant recommendations to users.

6.2 Collaborative Filtering

Collaborative filtering is a technique used in recommendation systems to predict user preferences based on the preferences of similar[1] users. It's a popular method because it doesn't rely on explicit information about items, making it suitable for various domains like movies, music, and products.

Types of Collaborative Filtering:

User-Based Collaborative Filtering:

Similarity Measure: Calculate the similarity between users based on their ratings or preferences for items.

Prediction: Predict a user's rating for an item by averaging the ratings of similar users for that item.

Item-Based Collaborative Filtering:

Similarity Measure: Calculate the similarity between items based on how users have rated them.

Prediction: Recommend items that are similar to items a user has liked.

Challenges and Limitations:

Cold Start Problem: Difficulty in making recommendations for new users or new items with limited ratings.

Sparsity: Most users only rate a small fraction of items, leading to sparse rating matrices.

Scalability: As the number of users and items grows, computational costs can increase.

Addressing Challenges:

Hybrid Approaches: Combine collaborative filtering with content-based filtering to improve recommendations.

Matrix Factorization: Reduce the dimensionality of the rating matrix to alleviate sparsity and improve scalability.

Contextual Factors: Consider contextual factors like time, location, and device to personalize recommendations.

By understanding the principles of collaborative filtering and addressing its limitations, you can build effective recommendation systems that provide personalized experiences for users.

6.3 Content-Based Filtering

Content-based filtering is a recommendation technique that suggests items to users based on their similarity to items the user has previously interacted with. It relies on analyzing the content or features of items to determine their relevance to a user's preferences.

How it works:

Item Representation: Each item is represented by a set of features or attributes, such as genre, director, keywords, or plot summary.

User Profile: A user profile is created based on the items they have interacted with. This profile can include a list of preferred features or a weighted vector representing the user's interests.

Similarity Calculation: The similarity between items and the user's profile is calculated using techniques like cosine similarity or Euclidean distance.

Recommendation: Items that are most similar to the user's profile are recommended.

Advantages of Content-Based Filtering:

No Cold Start Problem: It can recommend items to new users based on their explicit preferences.

Explainability: It can provide explanations for recommendations, as they are based on the content of items.

Novelty: It can discover new items that are similar to a user's preferences but haven't been rated yet.

Disadvantages of Content-Based Filtering:

Limited Recommendation Scope: It can only recommend items similar to those already known to the user.

Overspecialization: It may lead to a narrow range of recommendations, as the system may focus on specific features or genres.

Improving Content-Based Filtering:

Rich Feature Representation: Use rich and diverse features to represent items, such as textual, visual, and audio features.

Natural Language Processing: Employ NLP techniques to extract semantic meaning from text descriptions.

Hybrid Approaches: Combine content-based filtering with collaborative filtering to leverage the strengths of both techniques.

By effectively leveraging content-based filtering, you can provide personalized recommendations that cater to users' specific interests and preferences.

Chapter 7

Question Answering Systems

7.1 Understanding Question Answering

Question Answering (QA) is a field of artificial intelligence that aims to provide accurate and informative answers to user queries. It involves understanding the query, retrieving relevant information from a knowledge base, and generating a concise and informative response.

Key Components of a Question Answering System:

Natural Language Understanding (NLU):

Tokenization: Breaking down the query into words or tokens.

Part-of-Speech Tagging: Identifying the grammatical role of each word.

Named Entity Recognition (NER): Identifying entities like people, organizations, and locations.

Dependency Parsing: Analyzing the grammatical structure of the sentence.

Information Retrieval:

Document Retrieval: Identifying relevant documents from a knowledge base.

Passage Retrieval: Extracting relevant passages from the retrieved documents.

Answer Extraction:

Exact Match: Directly extracting the answer from the text.

Answer Generation: Generating a concise and informative answer using language models.

Response Generation:

Natural Language Generation (NLG): Constructing a coherent and grammatically correct response.

Formatting: Formatting the response appropriately, such as providing a list or a paragraph.

Challenges in Question Answering:

Ambiguity: Natural language can be ambiguous, leading to multiple interpretations of a query.

Contextual Understanding: Understanding the context of a query is crucial for accurate answers.

Knowledge Base Quality: The quality of the knowledge base significantly impacts the quality of answers.

Evaluation: Evaluating the quality of answers can be subjective and challenging.

Applications of Question Answering:

Chatbots and Virtual Assistants: Answering user queries in real-time.

Search Engines: Enhancing search results with direct answers.

Customer Service: Providing quick and accurate answers to customer inquiries.

Educational Tools: Answering student questions and explaining complex concepts.

By addressing these challenges and leveraging advanced techniques, question answering systems can provide valuable information and improve user experiences.

7.2 Building a Question Answering System

Building a question answering system involves several key steps:

1. Data Collection and Preprocessing

Gather Data: Collect a large corpus of text data relevant to your domain.

Data Cleaning: Remove noise, inconsistencies, and irrelevant information.

Tokenization: Break text into tokens (words or subwords).

Stop Word Removal: Remove common words that don't add much meaning.

Stemming or Lemmatization: Reduce words to their root form.

2. Document Understanding

Document Indexing: Create an index of documents for efficient retrieval.

Document Vectorization: Convert documents into numerical representations (embeddings) using techniques like BERT or other language models.

3. Query Understanding

Query Vectorization: Convert user queries into numerical vectors.

Intent Recognition: Identify the user's intent (e.g., factual question, yes/no question).

Entity Recognition: Identify entities in the query (e.g., people, places, organizations).

4. Passage Retrieval

Similarity Search: Use similarity search techniques (e.g., cosine similarity) to find relevant passages from the document index.

Ranking: Rank the retrieved passages based on relevance to the query.

5. Answer Extraction

Exact Match: Directly extract the answer from the relevant passage.

Reading Comprehension: Use techniques like attention mechanisms to understand the context of the passage and generate an answer.

6. Response Generation

Natural Language Generation: Generate a natural language response based on the extracted answer.

Formatting: Format the response appropriately (e.g., plain text, structured data).

Key Technologies and Libraries:

NLP Libraries: NLTK, spaCy, Hugging Face Transformers

Vector Database: Pinecone, Faiss, Milvus, Weaviate

Machine Learning Frameworks: TensorFlow, PyTorch

Search Engines: Elasticsearch, Algolia

Example using Hugging Face Transformers and Pinecone:

```python
Python
from transformers import AutoTokenizer,
AutoModelForQuestionAnswering
import pinecone

# Initialize Pinecone
pinecone.init(
    api_key="YOUR_API_KEY",
    environment="YOUR_ENVIRONMENT"
)

# Load the model
model_name = "distilbert-base-cased-distilled-squad"
tokenizer = AutoTokenizer.from_pretrained(model_name)
model                                                 =
AutoModelForQuestionAnswering.from_pretrained(model_name)

# Create a Pinecone index
pinecone.create_index(
    name="my-index",
    dimension=768,  # Dimension of document embeddings
    metric="CosineSimilarity"
)

# Vectorize documents and insert into Pinecone
```

```
# ...

# Process a user query
def answer_question(question):
    inputs = tokenizer(question, return_tensors="pt")
    with torch.no_grad():
        outputs = model(**inputs)

            start_scores,    end_scores    =    outputs.start_logits,
outputs.end_logits
    answer_start = torch.argmax(start_scores)
    answer_end = torch.argmax(end_scores) + 1

                                        answer              =
tokenizer.decode(inputs['input_ids'][0][answer_start:answer_end])
    return answer
```

By combining these techniques and leveraging powerful tools, you can build robust and accurate question answering systems.

7.3 Evaluating QA Performance

Evaluating the performance of a Question Answering (QA) system is crucial to measure its effectiveness and identify areas for improvement. Here are some key metrics and techniques to assess QA performance:

Objective Metrics:

Exact Match (EM): Measures the exact match between the generated answer and a reference answer.

F1-Score: Combines precision and recall to evaluate the overall accuracy of the system.

BLEU (Bilingual Evaluation Understudy): Evaluates the quality of generated text by comparing it to reference answers.

ROUGE (Recall-Oriented Understudy for Gisting Evaluation): Measures the overlap between generated and reference summaries.

METEOR (Metric for Evaluation of Translation with Explicit Ordering): Evaluates the similarity between generated and reference text, considering both word-level and sentence-level matching.

Subjective Metrics:

Human Evaluation: Human experts can assess the quality of answers based on factors like relevance, coherence, and comprehensiveness.

User Surveys: Gathering feedback from users can provide insights into user satisfaction and perceived quality.

Challenges in Evaluation:

Subjectivity: Human evaluation can be subjective, leading to variations in ratings.

Contextual Understanding: Evaluating the system's ability to understand context can be complex.

Factual Accuracy: Assessing the factual accuracy of answers requires access to reliable ground truth information.

Language Nuances: Handling language nuances and cultural differences can be challenging.

Improving QA Performance:

Data Quality: Ensure the quality and diversity of the training data.

Model Architecture: Experiment with different model architectures and hyperparameters.

Feature Engineering: Incorporate relevant features like named entity recognition, part-of-speech tagging, and sentiment analysis.

Regular Evaluation: Continuously evaluate the system's performance and identify areas for improvement.

User Feedback: Use user feedback to refine the system and address shortcomings.

Human-in-the-Loop: Consider incorporating human intervention to improve the quality of answers, especially for complex queries.

By carefully evaluating QA performance and implementing appropriate strategies, we can build more accurate and effective question answering systems. Would you like to delve deeper into a specific metric or technique?

Chapter 8

Anomaly Detection

8.1 Detecting Anomalies with Vector Databases

Vector databases can be a powerful tool for anomaly detection, especially when dealing with complex, high-dimensional data. Here's how:

Understanding Anomalies

An anomaly, or outlier, is a data point that deviates significantly from the norm. In the context of vector databases, anomalies can be identified by their distance from other data points in the vector space.

Techniques for Anomaly Detection with Vector Databases

Distance-Based Methods:

Euclidean Distance: Calculate the distance between a data point and its nearest neighbors.

Mahalanobis Distance: Considers the covariance matrix of the data to account for correlations between features.

Isolation Forest: Isolates anomalous data points by randomly partitioning the data space.

Density-Based Methods:

Local Outlier Factor (LOF): Measures the local deviation of a data point from its neighbors.

DBSCAN (Density-Based Spatial Clustering of Applications with Noise): Clusters high-density regions and identifies points as outliers if they don't belong to any cluster.

Clustering-Based Methods:

K-Means Clustering: Groups similar data points into clusters. Anomalies can be identified as points that don't belong to any cluster or are far from cluster centers.

One-Class Classification:

One-Class SVM: Trains a model to identify normal data points and flags outliers as those that fall outside the decision boundary.

Implementing Anomaly Detection with Vector Databases

Vectorize Data: Convert your data into numerical vectors.

Index Data: Store the vectors in a vector database.

Perform Similarity Search: Use the database to find the nearest neighbors for each data point.

Calculate Anomaly Scores: Use distance-based or density-based methods to calculate anomaly scores.

Set Threshold: Determine a threshold to identify data points as anomalies.

Example using Pinecone:

```python
Python
import pinecone

# Initialize Pinecone
pinecone.init(
```

```python
    api_key="YOUR_API_KEY",
    environment="YOUR_ENVIRONMENT"
)

# Create an index
pinecone.create_index(
    name="my-index",
    dimension=128,  # Dimension of your vectors
    metric="CosineSimilarity"
)

# Insert vectors
pinecone.upsert(
    index_name="my-index",
    vectors=[
        ("vector1", [1, 2, 3, ...]),
        ("vector2", [4, 5, 6, ...]),
        # ...
    ]
)

# Query for anomalies
query_vector = [10, 20, 30, ...]  # An anomalous vector
results = pinecone.query(
    index_name="my-index",
    vector=query_vector,
    top_k=10
)

# Calculate anomaly score based on distances to nearest
neighbors
```

By leveraging the efficient similarity search capabilities of vector databases, you can effectively identify anomalies in your data and take appropriate actions.

8.2 Anomaly Detection Techniques

Anomaly detection is a crucial task in data mining and machine learning, involving identifying data points that deviate significantly from the norm. Here are some common techniques used for anomaly detection:

Statistical Methods

Z-Score: Measures how many standard deviations a data point is from the mean.

Box Plot: Identifies outliers based on quartiles and interquartile range.

Histogram Analysis: Visualizes the distribution of data and identifies outliers as data points that fall outside the main distribution.

Machine Learning Methods

One-Class Support Vector Machine (OCSVM): Trains a model to identify normal data points and flags outliers as those that fall outside the decision boundary.

Isolation Forest: Isolates anomalous data points by randomly partitioning the data space.

Local Outlier Factor (LOF): Measures the local deviation of a data point from its neighbors.

Autoencoders: Trains a neural network to reconstruct input data. Anomalies are identified as data points that the model fails to reconstruct accurately.

Clustering-Based Methods

K-Means Clustering: Groups similar data points into clusters. Anomalies can be identified as points that don't belong to any cluster or are far from cluster centers.

DBSCAN (Density-Based Spatial Clustering of Applications with Noise): Groups together points that are closely packed together[1] (high-density regions). Points that are not part of any cluster are considered outliers.

Time Series Anomaly Detection

Statistical Methods: Use techniques like ARIMA, exponential smoothing, or statistical process control.

Machine Learning Methods: Employ time series forecasting models (e.g., LSTM, GRU) to predict future values and flag significant deviations.

Choosing the Right Technique

The choice of anomaly detection technique depends on several factors:

Data Type: Numerical, categorical, or time series data.

Data Distribution: Normal or skewed distribution.

Anomaly Type: Point anomalies, contextual anomalies, or collective anomalies.

Computational Resources: The complexity of the technique and the size of the dataset.

By understanding these techniques and considering the specific characteristics of your data, you can effectively detect anomalies and gain valuable insights from your data.

8.3 Real-World Applications of Anomaly Detection

Anomaly detection has a wide range of applications across various industries. Here are some real-world examples:

Finance

Fraud Detection: Identifying unusual spending patterns or transactions that may indicate fraudulent activity.

Network Intrusion Detection: Detecting abnormal network traffic that could signal a cyberattack.

Healthcare

Patient Monitoring: Identifying abnormal vital signs or medical test results that may indicate a health issue.

Medical Image Analysis: Detecting tumors or other abnormalities in medical images.

Manufacturing

Quality Control: Identifying defective products or anomalies in production processes.

Predictive Maintenance: Predicting equipment failures by detecting abnormal sensor readings.

IT Operations

System Monitoring: Detecting system failures, performance degradation, or security breaches.

Network Security: Identifying malicious network traffic or unusual user behavior.

E-commerce

Fraud Detection: Identifying fraudulent transactions or fake reviews.

Customer Behavior Analysis: Detecting unusual customer behavior that may indicate issues or opportunities.

Cybersecurity

Network Security: Detecting malicious network traffic, DDoS attacks, and other cyber threats.

Insider Threat Detection: Identifying unusual user behavior that may indicate insider threats.

Environmental Monitoring

Climate Change Analysis: Detecting unusual climate patterns or extreme weather events.

Pollution Monitoring: Identifying pollution spikes or unusual environmental conditions.

By effectively detecting anomalies, organizations can improve efficiency, reduce costs, and mitigate risks.

Chapter 9

Natural Language Processing

9.1 NLP and Vector Databases: A Powerful Combination

Natural Language Processing (NLP) and **Vector Databases** are two powerful technologies that, when combined, can revolutionize how we interact with and understand language.

How NLP and Vector Databases Work Together

Text to Vectors:

NLP techniques like word embeddings or sentence embeddings convert text into numerical representations (vectors).

Popular techniques include Word2Vec, GloVe, and BERT.

Vector Storage and Retrieval:

Vector databases efficiently store and retrieve these high-dimensional vectors.

They enable similarity search, allowing you to find semantically similar documents or passages.

Semantic Search:

Vector databases can power semantic search, where the search engine understands the meaning of queries and returns relevant results based on semantic similarity, not just keyword matching.

Key Applications

Semantic Search:

Finding relevant documents or information based on the meaning of the query.

Document Similarity:

Identifying similar documents to a given query or document.

Text Classification and Clustering:

Grouping similar documents or categorizing them based on their semantic content.

Sentiment Analysis:

Analyzing the sentiment of text (positive, negative, neutral).

Question Answering:

Understanding and answering complex questions.

Chatbots and Virtual Assistants:

Enabling more natural and context-aware conversations.

Benefits of Using Vector Databases for NLP

Efficient Similarity Search: Vector databases are optimized for similarity search, making them ideal for finding semantically similar text.

Scalability: They can handle large datasets and high-throughput queries.

Flexibility: They can store various types of embeddings, including word, sentence, and document embeddings.

Integration with Machine Learning: They can be easily integrated with machine learning pipelines for training and inference.

By combining the power of NLP and vector databases, you can build intelligent applications that can understand and process human language in a more sophisticated and efficient way.

9.2 Text Classification and Sentiment Analysis with Vector Databases

Text Classification and **Sentiment Analysis** are two fundamental tasks in Natural Language Processing (NLP) that can be significantly enhanced by using vector databases.

Text Classification

Text classification involves categorizing text into predefined classes or labels. Vector databases can be used to:

Vectorize Text: Convert text documents into numerical representations (vectors).

Train a Classifier: Train a machine learning model (e.g., SVM, Naive Bayes, or neural network) to classify text based on their vector representations

Store Model and Vectors: Store the trained model and document vectors in a vector database.

Classify New Text: Vectorize new text, query the database to find similar documents, and assign the most frequent class label.

Sentiment Analysis

Sentiment analysis determines the sentiment expressed in a piece of text (positive, negative, or neutral). Here's how vector databases can help:

Vectorize Text: Convert text into numerical representations.

Train a Sentiment Classifier: Train a model to classify text as positive, negative, or neutral.

Store Model and Vectors: Store the trained model and text vectors in a vector database.

Analyze New Text: Vectorize new text, query the database to find similar text, and assign the sentiment of the most similar text.

Vector Database Benefits for Text Classification and Sentiment Analysis

Efficient Similarity Search: Quickly find similar documents to new text.

Scalability: Handle large datasets and real-time analysis

Flexibility: Store various types of embeddings (word, sentence, document).

Integration with Machine Learning: Easily integrate with machine learning pipelines.

Example using Pinecone:

```python
Python
import pinecone
from sentence_transformers import SentenceTransformer

# Initialize Pinecone
```

```python
pinecone.init(
    api_key="YOUR_API_KEY",
    environment="YOUR_ENVIRONMENT"
)

# Create an index
pinecone.create_index(
    name="text_index",
    dimension=768,  # Dimension of sentence embeddings
    metric="CosineSimilarity"
)

# Vectorize text and insert into Pinecone
model = SentenceTransformer('all-MiniLM-L6-v2')
embeddings = model.encode(["This is a positive review.", "This is a negative review."])
pinecone.upsert(
    index_name="text_index",
    vectors=[
        ("text1", embeddings[0]),
        ("text2", embeddings[1])
    ]
)

# Classify new text
new_text = "This product is amazing!"
new_vector = model.encode([new_text])
results = pinecone.query(
    index_name="text_index",
    vector=new_vector,
    top_k=1
)

# Assign the sentiment of the most similar text
if results['matches'][0]['score'] > 0.8:
```

```
    print("Positive sentiment")
else:
    print("Negative sentiment")
```

By effectively combining NLP techniques and vector databases, you can build powerful text classification and sentiment analysis systems.

9.3 Text Generation and Summarization with Vector Databases

Text Generation and **Text Summarization** are two powerful NLP tasks that can be significantly enhanced by using vector databases.

Text Generation

Text generation involves creating new text, such as articles, poems, or code. Vector databases can be used to:

Generate Text Sequentially

Train a language model (e.g., GPT-3) to generate text one token at a time, conditioned on the previous tokens.

Use a vector database to store and retrieve relevant context from a large corpus of text.

Generate Text from Structured Data:

Convert structured data (e.g., tables, databases) into text.

Use vector databases to store and retrieve relevant information.

Text Summarization

Text summarization involves condensing long documents into shorter summaries. Vector databases can be used to:

Extract Key Sentences:

Identify the most important sentences in a document using techniques like TF-IDF or sentence embeddings.

Store these key sentences in a vector database.

Retrieve relevant sentences for a given query.

Generate Abstractive Summaries:

Use language models to generate concise summaries that capture the main ideas of a document.

Vector databases can be used to store and retrieve relevant context from a large corpus of text.

Vector Database Benefits for Text Generation and Summarization

Efficient Retrieval of Relevant Information: Vector databases can quickly retrieve relevant information from large datasets.

Improved Contextual Understanding: By storing and retrieving contextual information, vector databases can enhance the quality of generated text.

Scalability: Handle large datasets and real-time generation.

Flexibility: Store various types of embeddings (word, sentence, document).

Example using Hugging Face Transformers and Pinecone:

```python
Python
from transformers import pipeline
import pinecone

# Initialize Pinecone
pinecone.init(
    api_key="YOUR_API_KEY",
    environment="YOUR_ENVIRONMENT"
)

# Create an index
pinecone.create_index(
    name="text_index",
    dimension=768,  # Dimension of sentence embeddings
    metric="CosineSimilarity"
)

# Vectorize text and insert into Pinecone
# ...

# Generate text
generator = pipeline("text-generation", model="gpt2")
prompt = "Write a summary of the following text:"
generated_text = generator(prompt + " " + text)

# Summarize text
summarizer = pipeline("summarization")
summary = summarizer(text)
```

By combining the power of NLP techniques and vector databases, you can build advanced text generation and summarization systems.

Chapter 10

Future Trends and Best Practices

10.1 Emerging Trends in Vector Databases

Vector databases are rapidly evolving, with several exciting trends shaping the future of this technology:

1. Hybrid Search

Combining Semantic and Keyword Search: By integrating traditional keyword-based search with semantic search, hybrid search offers a more comprehensive and accurate search experience.

Enhanced User Experience: Hybrid search can better understand user intent and provide more relevant results.

2. Real-Time Analytics

Streaming Data: Vector databases are becoming increasingly capable of processing and analyzing streaming data in real-time

Time-Series Data: By representing time series data as vectors, anomaly detection and trend analysis can be performed efficiently.

3. Multi-Modal Search

Combining Text, Image, and Audio: Vector databases can be used to index and search across multiple modalities, enabling more powerful and flexible search capabilities.

Enhanced User Experience: Multi-modal search can provide more relevant and diverse results.

4. Federated Learning

Privacy-Preserving AI: By training models on decentralized data, federated learning can protect sensitive information.

Improved Model Performance: Federated learning can lead to more accurate and robust models.

5. Explainable AI

Understanding Model Decisions: By analyzing the vector representations and similarity metrics, it's possible to gain insights into how the model arrives at its decisions.

Building Trust: Explainable AI can help build trust in AI-powered systems.

6. Low-Code/No-Code Interfaces

Democratizing AI: User-friendly interfaces and pre-built pipelines make it easier for non-technical users to leverage vector databases.

Faster Time to Market: Low-code/no-code tools can accelerate the development of AI applications.

By staying updated on these emerging trends, you can leverage the full potential of vector databases to build innovative and powerful applications.

10.2 Best Practices for Vector Database Development

Here are some best practices to follow when developing applications with vector databases:

Data Preparation and Quality

Data Cleaning: Ensure data is clean and free of errors or inconsistencies.

Feature Engineering: Select or create relevant features that effectively represent the data.

Vectorization: Choose appropriate vectorization techniques (e.g., Word2Vec, BERT, CLIP) to create high-quality vector representations.

Index Selection and Tuning

Choose the Right Index: Select an index structure (e.g., HNSW, IVFFlat, Annoy) that is suitable for your specific use case and dataset.

Optimize Index Parameters: Fine-tune index parameters to balance accuracy and performance.

Dynamic Indexing: Consider using dynamic indexing techniques to update the index as new data is added or existing data changes.

Query Optimization

Query Filtering: Use metadata filters to reduce the search space and improve query performance.

Query Vector Quality: Ensure that the query vector is accurate and representative of the desired search intent.

Batch Queries: Process multiple queries simultaneously to improve efficiency.

Caching: Cache frequently accessed data to reduce query latency.

Monitoring and Optimization

Monitor Performance: Track query latency, throughput, and error rates.

Identify Bottlenecks: Analyze system logs and performance metrics to identify performance bottlenecks.

Optimize Index and Query Strategies: Adjust index parameters and query strategies to improve performance.

A/B Testing: Experiment with different configurations and techniques to find the optimal solution.

Security and Privacy

Data Encryption: Encrypt sensitive data at rest and in transit.

Access Controls: Implement robust access controls to protect sensitive data.

Compliance: Adhere to relevant data privacy regulations (e.g., GDPR, CCPA).

Ethical Considerations

Bias and Fairness: Be aware of potential biases in the data and models, and take steps to mitigate them.

Transparency: Make sure that the model's decision-making process is transparent and explainable.

Responsible AI: Use AI responsibly and ethically, avoiding harmful applications.

By following these best practices, you can build efficient, scalable, and reliable vector database applications that deliver high-quality results.

10.3 Ethical Considerations in AI and Vector Databases

As AI and vector databases become increasingly powerful, it's essential to consider the ethical implications of their development and deployment. Here are some key ethical considerations:

Bias and Fairness

Data Bias: Ensure that the data used to train AI models is representative and free from biases. Biased data can lead to biased models, which can perpetuate discrimination.

Algorithmic Bias: Be aware of the potential for algorithms to amplify biases present in the data.

Fairness Metrics: Use appropriate fairness metrics to assess the fairness of AI systems.

Privacy

Data Privacy: Protect user privacy by implementing robust data privacy practices, such as data minimization and anonymization.

Consent and Transparency: Obtain informed consent from users and be transparent about data collection and usage.

Security: Implement strong security measures to protect data from unauthorized access and breaches.

Transparency and Explainability

Model Interpretability: Develop techniques to understand how AI models make decisions.

Explainable AI: Make AI systems more transparent and understandable to humans.

Auditing and Monitoring: Regularly audit AI systems to identify and mitigate potential biases.

Accountability

Responsible Development: Develop AI systems with a sense of responsibility and accountability.

Ethical Guidelines: Adhere to ethical guidelines and principles for AI development.

Human Oversight: Ensure that human oversight is maintained to prevent unintended consequences.

Job Displacement and Economic Impact

Skill Development: Invest in education and training to help workers adapt to the changing job market.

Social Safety Nets: Implement social safety nets to support those affected by job displacement.

By addressing these ethical considerations, we can develop AI and vector database systems that are fair, transparent, and beneficial to society.